Trust me,
I'm a scientist

Pervez Hoodbhoy, Daniel Glaser, Steven Shapin

With an introduction by
Lloyd Anderson

Series editor
Rosemary Bechler

First published 2004
British Council
10 Spring Gardens
London SW1A 2BN
www.britishcouncil.org

Cover design by Atelier Works

© **British Council 2004** Design Department/R062/TBL
**The United Kingdom's international organisation for educational opportunities
and cultural relations.** We are registered in England as a charity.

Contents

Preface
by the Director-General

The British Council seeks to build long-term relationships between people of different cultures. Our currency is trust. The British Council has been a leader in cultural relations since its founding in 1934. In order to celebrate our 70th anniversary, I asked Counterpoint, our think tank on cultural relations, to commission a series of ten sets of essays, each set looking at a central issue from a variety of angles and viewpoints. The issues range from European enlargement to 'Britishness', and from the significance of death to the role of faith and the nature of secularism.

The 34 writers come from all over the world, though at least one in each set is British. Each introduction, with one exception, is written by a member of British Council staff. They testify to the richness of the intellectual and moral resource that the British Council represents.

Our intention is to stimulate debate rather than arrive at consensus. Some essays are controversial. None of them expresses, individually, a British Council viewpoint. They are the work of individual authors of distinction from whom we have sought views. But collectively, they represent something more than the sum of their parts – a commitment to the belief that dialogue is the essential heart of cultural relations.

Dialogue requires and generates trust. The biggest danger in what is often called public diplomacy work is that we simply broadcast views, policies, values and positions. A senior European diplomat recently said at a British Council conference: 'The world is fed up with hearing us talk. What it wants is for us to shut up and listen.' Listening and demonstrating our commitment to the free and creative interplay of ideas is an indispensable pre-condition for building trust.

To build trust we must engage in effective, open dialogue. Increased mutual understanding based on trust, whether we agree or disagree, is a precious outcome.

David Green KCMG

Introduction

Lloyd Anderson

Eric Hobsbawm, in 1994, wrote, 'No period in history has been more penetrated by and more dependent on natural sciences than the 20th century. Yet no period, since Galileo's recantation, has been less at ease with it. This is the paradox with which [we] must grapple . . . the progress of the natural sciences took place against a background glow of suspicion and fear.'

In conversation with Antonio Polito five years on, Hobsbawm was asked: 'Doesn't the power of science frighten you? The possibilities of cloning human beings, crossing animal and vegetable genes in a tomato?' He replied: 'Of course it frightens me . . . if there was some guarantee that the persons who make these developments possible also knew what to do with them, how to use them, and when not to use them at all, I would be less frightened.'

And the political dimension in this state of affairs is added to by David Marquand, writing in *The Guardian* about public servants and the social democratic tradition. He remarks that 'incessant marketisation has done even more damage [to public services] than low taxation and resource starvation. It has generated a culture of distrust, which is nibbling away at the values of professionalism, citizenship, equity and service like an acrid fog. For the marketisers . . . there is no point in appealing to the values of common citizenship [because] there are no citizens; there are only consumers.'

Do I trust scientists? Let's deal first with trust in scientific practice. If I heard a scientist on the radio say 'this is one hundred per cent safe' or 'that is not possible', I simply wouldn't believe him or her. And if I was sufficiently provoked by the scientist's categorical statements, I would track down the published data and try to make a decision for myself (and Daniel Glaser's essay highlights a number of questions around this). If, however, the scientist said 'there is no unequivocal answer, but our research shows that in x out of y cases this drug reduces the risk of z', I probably would believe it. But, of course, there are lots of issues to consider here.

I am scientifically trained and so, fortunately, can try to interpret the data and methodology for myself. Science is about the weight of evidence, and one can only ever prove that something isn't the case. Thus one can never say 'all storks are white' because one cannot examine the colour of every stork in existence. But, on seeing a black stork, one can immediately say 'not all storks are white'.

Yet we want categorical answers to questions such as 'is genetically engineered food safe?' or 'will this mobile phone damage my child's brain?' The truthful answer is 'we don't know for sure' because the answer must be based on probability and available evidence, but the public and the media and politicians more often want a straightforward 'yes' or 'no' and see anything else as prevarication. This is contrary, given that everyone taking part in a scientific discussion should be open to the possibility of being persuaded by an opposing argument or new evidence.

And then the scientist might say 'we can't be sure but at present there is no evidence to suggest this disease is transmitted through the food we eat' and the politician selectively hears 'this food is safe to eat' (with the neat option of blaming scientific advice when the going gets tough). If we look at the BSE crisis, the scientists did say 'we don't know', but the politicians, fearing panic and collapse of the beef market, interpreted this as 'there's nothing obviously wrong, so it must be safe'.

Here we are starting to drift away from scientific practice towards the suspicion of vested interests at play and the demand for openness and accountability (as both Daniel Glaser and Steven Shapin draw attention to). During the Stalinist era there was total correspondence between political and scientific statements at all times, reflecting the power of political authority over scientific announcements. Hobsbawm (1997) argues that people ought to be partisan in their attitude to the sciences, because the sciences themselves are partisan. The possibility of a purely objective and value-free science is naïve.

This brings us to a third issue, where the scientist says 'this research will help society' but someone else applies the knowledge in ways the scientist never imagined, often in the pursuit of power or profit (as Pervez Hoodbhoy mentions in his essay). We may distrust the way that scientific results and discoveries will be used; in other words the technological pathways taken. For example, multinational companies introduce new foods, the benefits of which (longer shelf-life) accrue to them while the (unknown) risks are taken by the consumer (and Steven Shapin notes Monsanto's experience in this context).

As an aside, a book on Manchester, written by Dave Haslam, starts by looking at the history of the first urban city, built around cotton. The word 'Luddite' commonly refers to someone who is anti-technology or progress, yet Haslam argues that the Luddites smashed up the machinery that the cotton-mill owners were introducing because the machines were dangerous and people were losing fingers, eyes and arms, and getting no more pay than before. The mill workers were taking the risks while the benefits accrued to the mill owners. Is this so very different to consumers voting with their shopping trolleys in the supermarket, rejecting genetically modified tomatoes with a longer shelf-life in favour of the organic food section?

In 2000 the British Council organised, for the government, an international conference on science communication in London, honouring a commitment made by the then Minister for International Development at the World Science Conference in Budapest, to explore the role of science communication in assisting societal and scientific progress. This followed on from a successful series of public debates in nine cities around the world called 'Towards a Democratic Science', which looked at perceptions of science, the assessment of risk, the need for regulation, ethical responsibility, public consultation and consumer protection.

The public debates were linked together by a global e-forum, where 600 people discussed think pieces posted by the speakers taking part in the live debates overseas. It appeared, in virtual space, as if there were two tribes, so removed from each other that they had begun to speak different languages. The divide was not about anything as simple as being pro- or anti-science, however. The differences were less clearly articulated and more instinctive than that. One side tended to see scientists as pathfinders, finding a way for the rest of society to follow, while the other side talked about society setting the broader agenda which science should duly serve, even if the implication was that scientists should submit to increased social control. The gulf between these two tribes colours all efforts to forge a democratic science.

We followed up the public debates and e-forum with a pioneering international seminar on democratic science in March 2001, which was attended by policy-makers, scientists, media people and research managers from developed, developing and transitional countries. The participants felt that a democratic science is about innovation with respect to the needs of the many, not just the most powerful few. It recognises that the decisions made about the use of scientific knowledge and new technologies can't be left to scientists – nor indeed, to any one section of society – without excluding certain communities from the social, economic and cultural benefits that others then enjoy. Democratic science strategies and policies aim to ensure that the needs and wishes of all communities become embodied in scientific pathways and technological developments.

The public – indeed, the many publics – are not anti-science. Rather, they are sceptical about the decisions that are being made on their behalf about scientific developments; decisions they know will be influenced – to a greater or lesser extent – by economic and political interests. Mistrust and scepticism about science and the possible technological pathways are not necessarily unjustified.

Returning to the scientists, they must dare to state the evidence honestly, despite the pressures placed on them by institutions, funders, politicians and the media. Nothing in science is completely right; it's just that it has not yet been proved wrong.

Returning science to Islam – the rocky road ahead

Pervez Hoodbhoy

On the morning of the first Gulf War in 1991, having just heard the news of the US attack on Baghdad, I walked into my office in the physics department in a state of numbness and depression. Mass death and devastation would surely follow. I was dismayed, but not surprised, to discover my PhD student, a militant activist of the Jamaat-i-Islami's student wing in Islamabad, in a state of euphoria. Islam's victory, he said, is inevitable because God is on our side and the Americans cannot survive without alcohol and women. He reasoned that neither would be available in Iraq, and happily concluded that the Americans were doomed. Two weeks later, after the rout of Saddam's army and 70,000 dead Iraqis, I reminded him of his words. He had nothing to say.

But years later, soon after earning a reasonably good doctorate in quantum field theory and elementary particles, he quit academia and put his considerable physics skills to use in a very different direction. Today he heads a department that deals with missile guidance systems inside a liberally funded, massively sized defence organisation employing thousands to make nuclear weapons and missiles. Serving Pakistan and Islam, as he sees it, gives him a feeling of pride. Plus it pays about three times as much as a university job.

Technology is very welcome

In modern times every form of intellectual endeavour in Islam stands in poor health. Science, in particular, is almost nowhere to be seen. None the less, several Muslim countries have aimed for nuclear weapons and the highest kinds of technology. As the little episode above illustrates, defence technology is accorded top priority and has been more successful than science. The emphasis is reflected not just in salaries but also in research funding and social status. The nexus between technology and defence is made at a student's early stages of development. For example, freshmen at the elite Lahore University of Management Sciences are introduced to the fundamentals of computer science with the following textbook preface: 'It is military prowess that bestows technical and economic superiority to nations, and it is not otherwise. The association of science and technology with ruling empires is, therefore, natural.'

Technological nationalism – the association of power and national greatness with technology – finds its expression in the yearly celebration of Pakistan's nuclear achievements. While Iraq, Iran, and Libya have actively sought to make nuclear weapons, Pakistan is the only Muslim country to have achieved this goal. Since May 1998 the Pakistani state has flaunted its nuclear potency publicly, proudly, and provocatively. Nuclear shrines, erected with government funds, dot the country. One – a fibre glass model of the nuclear-blasted Chaghi Mountain – stands at the entrance to Islamabad, bathed at night in a garish, orange light. Officialdom has vigorously promoted nuclearisation as the symbol of Pakistan's high scientific achievement, national determination, self-respect, and the harbinger of a new Muslim era. Pakistan's Islamic parties rushed to claim ownership after the nuclear tests, seeing in the Bomb a sure sign of a reversal of fortunes, and a panacea for the ills that have plagued Muslims since the end of the Golden Age of Islam many centuries ago. Their hero was (and largely remains) Dr Abdul Qadeer Khan, a metallurgist with intimate knowledge of uranium enrichment technology acquired during his stint in Holland with URENCO, a European uranium enrichment consortium. Abdus Salam, the Nobel prize-winner of theoretical physics, remains largely unknown.

Technology was surrounded by religious taboos in earlier times.

But it is rapidly gaining acceptance in Muslim societies and earlier restrictions seem virtually incomprehensible to Muslims today. Public clocks had been banned in 16th-century Turkey under the Ottomans; the printing press was roundly condemned by the orthodox *ulema* in Muhammad Ali's Egypt; loudspeakers (even for the call to prayers) were once disallowed on religious grounds on the Indian subcontinent; and so forth. Some prohibitions still stand, but are rapidly weakening. Today prohibitions on blood transfusions and organ transplants are generally disregarded everywhere in the Muslim world in spite of orthodox restrictions. Television under the Taliban was severely restricted but has made its way into Muslim homes almost everywhere. In fact, technological innovation – even in matters relating to religious practices and rituals – is now welcomed by a growing consumerist middle class. Commercially available devices include Islamic screen savers and computerised holy texts, cell phones with GPS indicators indicating the direction towards *qibla*, prayer mats with sensors that keep count of the number of kneel-downs and head-downs for the forgetful; and electronically recorded voices that help in remembering the 99 names of Allah.

Science remains problematic
Islam's relationship with science, on the other hand, is less comfortable. To remove possible ambiguities, let me define 'science': it is the process wherein knowledge about the physical world is acquired in a systematic and logically self-consistent manner by observation, experimentation, testing of hypotheses, and observer-independent verification.

Some Muslims bristle at the very suggestion that there might be a disjuncture between Islam and science. A common reaction is to point towards the debt owed by modern science to the achievements of their ancestors. Indeed, Muslim intellectual giants such as Omar Khayyam, Jabir Ibn Hayyan, and Alhazen, are rightly remembered for their front-ranking intellectual achievements. But this does not solve the compatibility issue: it is a mistake to think that modern science is simply a more advanced form of ancient science. The two are separated by fundamentally different goals and world views.

In ancient times, science was a matter of discovering curious and interesting new phenomena and facts. These would sometimes tickle the fancy of kings and caliphs, and make the scholar rich or famous. The relation of science with technology was a distant one – a scientific discovery would only rarely result in the creation of new implements or tools, weapons of war, or new architectural methods and designs. Most importantly, given the state of knowledge in pre-modern times, it was simply not possible to have today's view of the universe wherein every physical phenomenon is traceable to physical principles. Modern science insists that these laws are rationally comprehensible, and have validity far beyond the situation from which they were deduced. For example, the laws of physics governing the motion of a falling stone are identical to those that determine the motion of a spacecraft travelling to Venus. These very laws also determine the manner in which DNA replicates, cells divide, or electric signals communicate information inside a computer. In this modern view, the human body is undoubtedly an immensely complex mechanical and electrical system. However, every part can be fully understood in terms of biological, chemical, and physical processes.

Modern scientific thought clearly comes with a high price tag. Before the Lutheran Reformation, this provoked a bitter battle between its adherents and the Church. In contemporary Islam, where there is no formal centre of religious authority, the reactions have been more varied.

Fortunately, the dominant Muslim response to the issue of the compatibility of science with Islam is a rather sensible one – that of indifference. Most Muslims are quite content with a vague belief that there is consistency rather than conflict. This is helped by the generally held view that science is a conglomeration of techniques, formulae, equipment, and machines. At best, science creates new gadgets and even jobs. At worst, it is something technical, which is dreadfully boring and difficult to learn. In any case, the reasoning goes, it is better not to worry excessively over arcane matters.

But others will not let sleeping dogs lie. In recent years the applications, methodology and epistemology of modern science have been severely criticised by growing numbers of Muslim academics. At one level, these are familiar postmodernist arguments: the development and application of a science that claims to be value-free is held to be the prime cause of the myriad problems facing the world today – weapons of mass destruction, environmental degradation, global inequities in the distribution of wealth and power, alienation of the individual, and so forth.

At another level, many orthodox Muslims reject the scientific method as well as the notion of science as knowledge. Knowledge for the sake of knowledge is declared to be dangerous and illegitimate; the only form of legitimate knowledge is that which leads to a greater understanding of the Divine. Daily television broadcasts, and hugely popular Muslim websites and books, resound with claims that exegesis of the Qur'an and a 'proper understanding' of the Arabic language can lead to every scientific discovery from human embryology and cerebral physiology to black holes and the expanding universe.

American universities are host to countless speakers who condemn modern science on Islamic grounds. Iranian-born scholar Seyyed Hossein Nasr, who commands $5,000 speaking fees, is often invited by campus Islamic groups. In a speech given at MIT that I found on the web, he argued that the Arabic word *ilm*, whose pursuit is a religious duty, has been wilfully applied to science and secular learning by Muslim modernists in an effort to make them more acceptable in Islamic societies. But science is subversion, he announces, 'because ever since children began to learn Lavoisier's Law that water is composed of oxygen and hydrogen, in many

Islamic countries they came home that evening and stopped saying their prayers'. In 1983, Nasr advised the Saudi government not to build a science museum because 'it could be a time bomb' and destroy faith in Islam.

A widening divide
My last Google keyword search on 'Islam and science' yielded 165,143 entries. These included hundreds of elaborately designed Islamic websites, some with counter hits running into tens of thousands. The one most frequently visited has a banner: 'Recently discovered astounding scientific facts, accurately described in the Muslim Holy Book and by the Prophet Muhammad (PBUH) 14 centuries ago.' Many seek to show that the birth of modern science would have been impossible but for Islam and Muslims. On the anti-science front there are familiar 19th-century arguments against Darwinism, with Harun Yahya of Turkey as the new Bishop Wilberforce.

I could not, however, find any websites dealing with the philosophical implications of the theory of relativity, quantum mechanics, chaos theory, strings or stem cells. Antiquity alone seems to matter. A visitor exits with the feeling that history's clock broke down somewhere during the 14th century and that plans for repair, at best, are vague.

In lieu of actual science, bizarre theories under the rubric of 'Islamic science' abound. Sometimes these are proposed by men with considerable technical skill. For example, Sultan Bashiruddin Mahmood, the first director of Pakistan's famous uranium enrichment plant, the Kahuta Research Laboratory (KRL) near Islamabad, the principal facility in the nuclear weapons complex, was given a major national honour for his contribution. This includes having several nuclear technology patents to his name. In addition, he was one of the chief designers of Pakistan's nuclear weapons plutonium production reactor at Khushab. For many years, Mahmood also ran the Holy Qur'an Research Foundation in Islamabad and drew up theories that he claimed to be founded in Islamic wisdom. He argued, for example, that capturing heavenly genies (said to be made out of fire by God) would provide the ideal fuel for solving Pakistan's energy problems. Mahmood and I had an acrimonious public debate in 1988 after he published his book *Mechanics of Doomsday and Life after Death,* in which he discussed the physics of souls and their electromagnetic properties. After 9/11, he shot into worldwide prominence upon the discovery of his contacts with the Taliban and Osama bin Laden.

It is not just science that stands in such poor health today. In a stunning indictment of the state of the Arab world, the *Arab Human Development Report 2002*, written by Arab intellectuals and released in Cairo, concluded that Arab societies are crippled by a lack of political freedom and knowledge. High-quality, mind-opening education is virtually non-existent. Half of all Arab women cannot read or write. The facts point to a bleak situation: 'The entire Arab world translates about 330 books annually, one-fifth the number that Greece translates,' says the survey. It adds that in the 1,000 years since the reign of the Caliph Maa'moun the Arabs have translated as many books as Spain translates in just one year.

The 2003 report was no less scathing: 'Almost all Arab countries have relinquished important knowledge-intensive aspects of oil production to foreign firms,' say the authors. 'The consequences of this abdication are severe.' They note that the divide between Arab countries and knowledge-based societies continues to widen.

Closer to home: in Pakistan, the commonly referred to 'crisis' of higher education understates the situation. Pakistan's public (and all but a handful of private) universities are intellectual rubble; their degrees of little consequence. With a population of 150 million, Pakistan has fewer than 20 computer scientists of sufficient calibre even to have a chance of getting tenure-track faculty positions at some B-grade US university. In physics, even if one roped in every good physicist in the country, it would still not be possible to staff one single proper department of physics. Mathematics is yet more impoverished: to claim that there are even five able mathematicians in Pakistan would be exaggerating their numbers. According to the Pakistan Council for Science and Technology, Pakistanis have succeeded in registering only eight patents internationally in 57 years. The state of the social sciences is scarcely better.

Not surprisingly, the teaching of modern science in schools and universities in Muslim countries (Iran, Turkey and Malaysia are exceptions) is generally very different from that in Western countries. Students are brought up to uncritically respect authority, and efficiently memorise and reproduce formulae and facts. Many of my department's graduate students write the magical inscription '786' on their exam sheets; others spend long hours praying before examinations. The general ambience in educational institutions has becoming progressively more conservative. A first-time visitor to my university's physics department in Islamabad (reputedly the best in Pakistan) innocently asked me if this was the Islamic Studies department. He had good reason to be confused: young burqa-clad women students were chanting something (actually, formulae for a physics test) with only their eyes visible from behind all-enveloping black shrouds. Brought up to respect authority uncritically, the only skill some of the students have is to efficiently memorise and reproduce formulae and facts, as if they were scripture. Instructions posted on the walls specify the proper prayer to use while ascending and descending the stairs; sayings of the Prophet have been posted all around; and there is scarcely anything related to physics on the noticeboards.

Iran and Turkey offer some relief in an otherwise bleak situation. Their universities and schools appear to be qualitatively better, and scientific research more fruitful and advanced. Nevertheless, flipping through scientific journals one seldom encounters a Muslim name. Muslims are conspicuous by their absence from the world of ideas and scholarship. An exception was Professor Abdus Salam who, together with Americans Steven Weinberg and Sheldon Glashow, won the Nobel Prize for physics in 1979. Salam was a remarkable man, in love with his country and religion. But although he was born a Muslim, he died a non-Muslim because the Ahmadi sect to which he belonged was expelled from Islam by an act of the Pakistani parliament in 1974.

Is a Muslim renaissance around the corner?
'Now Muslim leaders are planning [science's] revival and hope to restore a golden age', says Ziauddin Sardar, writer on Islam and contemporary cultural and scientific issues, in an optimistic article published recently in the *New Statesman*. Brave words, but I can see no visible evidence of significant collective activity, much less steps towards a 'golden age'. Visiting the websites of the Islamic Academy of Sciences (IAS), the Islamic Education, Scientific and Cultural Organisation (ISESCO) and the Organisation of Islamic Conference Standing Committee on Scientific and Technological Co-operation (COMSTECH), one learns that the sum of their combined activities over the last decade amount to sporadic conferences on disparate subjects, a handful of research and travel grants, and pitifully small sums for repair of equipment and spare parts. Lavish conferences have become an annual feature in Islamabad, with routine exhortations to develop science and technology for the *ummah*.

At the level of individual countries, there is more promise. An extraordinarily dynamic individual, Dr Atta-ur-Rahman, who is Pakistan's Minister for Science and Technology, was able to persuade the government to increase his ministry's budget over a three-year period, by a whopping factor of 60 (6,000 per cent) and the higher education budget by 12 (1,200 per cent). In consequence, a large human resource development plan for training teachers and researchers has been launched; internet connectivity in Pakistan has been substantially expanded; infrastructural improvements in universities and research institutions have been made; and a huge increase in faculty salaries is in the pipeline. Pakistan may well be unique: when I asked Dr Rahman, who also heads COMSTECH, if any of his ministerial counterparts in other Muslim countries felt a similar sense of urgency, he sadly shook his head.

The frequent exhortations and unprecedented attention to science and technology in Pakistan, as well as some parts of the Muslim world, are welcome. But will they work?

Noticeably absent is the call for critical thinking, scepticism, and the scientific method. But here lies the crux of the problem: science is about ideas, the flight of the imagination, and the unsparing rigour of logic and empirical testing. It is not primarily about resources for laboratories and equipment. The most powerful engines of science - mathematics and theoretical physics – are also the most parsimonious and undemanding of resources. Yet, with only modest exceptions, theoretical and foundational science is all but gone from Islamic lands. It is already evident that the huge science budget increase in Pakistan is also leading to massive wastage. Clearly money and resources are a relatively small part of the solution. We need to probe deeper.

A brilliant past that vanished

Taking refuge in the past is sad but understandable. Unlike the native peoples of South America or Africa, Muslims have a rich history of contributing to science and, to an extent, technology as well. Martians visiting Earth in the Golden Age of Islam, between the 9th and 13th-centuries would surely have reported back to headquarters that the only people doing decent work in science, philosophy or medicine were Muslims. Muslims not only preserved the ancient learning of the Greeks, they also made substantial innovations.

Science flourished in the Golden Age because of a strong rationalist and liberal tradition, carried on by a group of Muslim thinkers known as the Mutazilites. To the extent that they were able to dominate the traditionalists, progress was rapid. But in the 12th century, Muslim orthodoxy reawakened, spearheaded by the

Arab cleric Imam Al-Ghazali, who championed revelation over reason, and predestination over free will. Al-Ghazali damned mathematics as hostile to Islam; an intoxicant of the mind that weakened faith.

Caught in the iron grip of orthodoxy, Islam eventually choked. The bin Ladens and Mullah Omars of antiquity levelled the impressive edifice of Islamic cultural and scientific achievements. For petty doctrinal reasons, zealots persecuted and hounded those very Muslim scholars to whom Islamic civilisation owes much of its former brilliance and greatness. Al Kindi was whipped in public by a fanatical sultan and blinded; Al Razi and Ibn Sina escaped numerous charges of blasphemy and attempts upon their lives; and Ibn Rushd was exiled and had his books burned. It was also the end of tolerance, intellect and science in the Muslim world.

Meanwhile, the rest of the world moved on. The Renaissance brought an explosion of scientific enquiry in the West. This owed much to translations of Greek works carried out by Arabs, as well as original Muslim contributions in science, medicine, and philosophy. But the age of Arab cultural vitality and military dominance was on the way out. Mercantile capitalism and technological progress drove Western countries, in ways that were often brutal and at times genocidal, to colonise rapidly the Muslim world from Indonesia to Morocco.

The rise and fall of Muslim modernisation
The 19th-and early 20th-centuries saw a modest revival of efforts to bring science back into Islam. It had become clear, at least to a part of the Muslim elites in colonised countries, that they were paying a heavy price for not possessing the analytical tools of modern science and the associated social and political values of modern culture. Therefore, despite resistance from the orthodox, the logic of modernity found 19th-century Muslim adherents. Modernisers such as Mohammed Abduh and Rashid Rida of Egypt, Sayyed Ahmad Khan of India, and Jamaluddin Afghani (who belonged everywhere),

wished to adapt Islam to the times, interpret the Qur'an in ways consistent with modern science, and discard the Hadith (ways of the Prophet) in favour of the Qur'an. Others seized on the modern idea of the nation state.

When new nation states emerged in the 20th century, not a single leader was a fundamentalist. Turkey's Kemal Ataturk, Algeria's Ahmed Ben Bella, Indonesia's Sukarno, Pakistan's Muhammad Ali Jinnah, Egypt's Gamal Abdel Nasser, and Iran's Mohammed Mosaddeq all sought to organise their societies on the basis of secular values. However, Muslim and Arab nationalism, part of a larger anti-colonial nationalist current across the developing world, included the desire to control and deploy national resources for domestic benefit.

The conflict with Western greed was inevitable. Indeed, America's foes during the 1950s and 1960s were precisely these secular nationalists. Mossadeq, who opposed Standard Oil's grab at Iran's oil resources, was removed by a CIA coup. Sukarno, accused of being a communist, was overthrown by US intervention, with a resulting bloodbath that consumed about 800,000 lives. Nasser, who had Islamic fundamentalists like Saiyyid Qutb publicly executed, fell foul of the USA and Britain after the Suez Crisis. On the other hand, until 9/11, America's friends were the sheikhs of Saudi Arabia and the Gulf states, all of whom practised highly conservative forms of Islam, but were strongly favoured by Western oil interests.

Pressed from outside, corrupt and incompetent from within, secular Muslim governments proved unable to defend national interests or deliver social justice. Such failures left a vacuum that Islamic religious movements grew to fill – in Iran, Pakistan and Sudan, to name a few. The times had begun to change, but what was only a trot became a gallop in 1979 when Ronald Reagan's America entered a final stage of Cold War hostilities with the Soviet Union, aided by Pakistan and Saudi Arabia, who helped bring in some of the fiercest, most ideologically hardened, Islamic warriors from around the Arab world.

After the Soviet Union collapsed, the United States walked away from an Afghanistan in shambles. The Taliban emerged; Osama bin Laden and his al-Qa'ida made Afghanistan their base. September 11 followed. The subsequent vengeance extracted by the USA against Afghanistan, Iraq, and Palestine, was radically to change the relationship of Islam with the West. The two Gulf Wars, televised in exultant detail, revealed the Arabs as a crippled, powerless mass. When Israeli bulldozers levelled entire neighbourhoods of Jenin and Rafah, and American soldiers tortured and sexually abused the inmates of Abu Ghraib, Arabs could do no more than impotently rail at their enemies. The lure of Islamic fundamentalism provided an escape from bitter realities and the promise of ultimate victory.

The modernisation and secularisation of Muslim countries that had seemed inevitable just a half-century ago, has been indefinitely postponed in the wake of 9/11, and particularly the latest conflict in Iraq. Many in the Muslim world ascribe these reversals solely to America's imperial actions (and, earlier, those of Europe). But this is only one contributing factor, albeit an important one. The extreme difficulty of adapting to a post-Renaissance, knowledge-based society is also due to a belief system that is remarkably resistant to change.

Will it rain if you pray?
Questions hovering over science and Islam will not go away. Take the issue of miracles: does God suspend the laws of physics in response to the actions of human beings? Following the lead of Renaissance thinkers, Muslim reformers of the 19th century, such as Syed Ahmad Khan, argued that miracles must be understood in broad allegorical terms rather than literally. Following the Mutazillite tradition, they insisted on an interpretation of the Qu'ran that was in conformity with the observed truths of science, thereby doing away with such commonly held beliefs as the Great Flood and Adam's descent from

heaven. It was a risky proposition, and one that has been wilfully forgotten in our times.

Miracles of all sorts continue to be sought. For example, whenever there is a drought in Pakistan, every head of state from General Zia-ul-Haq to General Pervez Musharraf, together with their governors and chief ministers, have joined with the *ulema* in asking the public to come out in large numbers and perform the prescribed *namaz-i-istisqa* (prayer for rain). Millions comply.

My allusion to this issue in a seminar where I described rain as a physical process uninfluenced by divine forces drew an angry reaction from a professor, who is also an influential religious authority at the elite Lahore University of Management Sciences, possibly the most liberal university in Pakistan. All students received an e-mail, part of which is reproduced below:

> 'The fact that rainfall sometimes is caused in response to prayers is a matter of human experience. Although I cannot narrate an incident directly, I know [this] from the observations of people who would not exaggerate. The problem is that Dr Hoodbhoy has narrowed down his mind to be influenced by only those facts that could be explained by the cause-and-effect relationship. That's a classic example of academic prejudice . . . our world is not running on the principle of a causal relationship. It is running the way it is being run by its Master. Man has discovered that, generally speaking, the physical phenomena of our world follow the principle of cause and effect. However, that may not always happen, because the One who is running it has never committed Himself to stick to that principle.

I responded with the following points:

■ Dr Zaheer admits that he has never personally witnessed rainfall in consequence to prayers, but confidently states that this is 'a matter of human experience' because he thinks some others have seen unusual things happen. Well, there are people who are willing to swear on oath that they have seen Elvis's ghost. Others claim that they have seen UFOs, horned beasts, apparitions and the dead arise. Without disputing that some of these people might be sincere and honest, I must emphasise that science cannot agree to this methodology. There is no limit to the power of people's imagination. Unless these mysterious events are recorded on camera, we cannot accept them as factual occurrences.

- Rain is a physical process (evaporation, cloud formation, nucleation and condensation). It is complicated, because the atmospheric motion of gases needs many variables for a proper description. However, it obeys exactly the same physical laws as deduced by looking at gases in a cylinder, falling bodies, and so forth. Personally I would be most interested to know whether prayers can also cause the reversal of much simpler kinds of physical processes. For example, can a stone be made to fall upward instead of downward? Or can heat be made to flow from a cold body to a hot body by appropriate spiritual prompting? If prayers can cause rain to fall from a blue sky, then all physics and all science deserves to be trashed.

- I am afraid that the track record for Dr Zaheer's point of view on rain is not very good. Saudi Arabia remains a desert in spite of its evident holiness, and the poor peasants of Sind have a terrible time with drought in spite of their simplicity and piety. Geography, not earnestness of prayer, appears to be the determining factor.

- Confidence in the cause-and-effect relationship is indeed the very foundation of science and, as a scientist, I fully stand by it. Press the letter 'T' on your keyboard and the same letter appears on the screen; step on the accelerator and your car accelerates; jump out of a window and you get hurt; put your hand on a stove and you get burnt. Those who doubt cause and effect do so at great personal peril.

■ Dr Zaheer is correct in saying that many different people (not just Muslims alone) believe they can influence physical events by persuading a divine authority. Indeed, in the specific context of rain-making, we have several examples. Red Indians had their very elaborate dances to please the Rain God; people of the African bush tribes beat drums and chant; and orthodox Hindus plead with Ram through spectacular *yagas* with hundreds of thousands of the faithful. Their methods seem a little odd to me, but I wonder if Dr Zaheer wishes to accord them respect and legitimacy.

Can Islam and science live together again?

The reader who wishes to get to the bottom line will be disappointed. There is no universally accepted answer, and there cannot be one. Unlike Christianity, in Islam there is no Vatican and no Pope. In the absence of a central authority, Muslims have greater flexibility to decide on theological and doctrinal issues.

The questions posed above can be asked of any religion. For purposes of discussion, it is useful to split every religion into four components. Science has no problem with the first three – they are matters of faith and individual choice:

■ **Metaphysical:** This relates to the particular beliefs of religion. Every faith has specific positions on issues as monotheism and polytheism, death and reincarnation, heaven and hell, prophets and holy men and rituals and relics.

■ **Ethical and moral:** Religions have a specific prescription of how individuals are expected to order their lives and why they have been brought into being. Conversely, science offers no guidance in determining right from wrong, and does not provide a reason for the existence of individuals or the human race. It is silent on eugenics or cloning, and polygamy or polyandry.

- **Inspirational and emotional:** Marmaduke Pickthall, who translated the Qu'ran into English, wrote of how the melody of its verses could move men to tears. Abdus Salam, transfixed by the symmetry of Lahore's Badshahi Mosque, said that it inspired him to think of the famous SU(2)xU(1) symmetry that revolutionised the world of particle physics.
- **Beliefs about the physical world:** There is a definite problem here: taken literally, the texts of all religions lead to a description of physical reality that belongs to antiquity and is definitely at odds with modern science. The issues are well known: the origin of life, non-material beings such as spirits and djinns, geocentricity, the nature of comets and meteors, and miracles such as the Great Flood and the parting of the Red Sea.

Let us provisionally accept the argument that the religious impulse propelled science in Muslim civilisation in its Golden Age through requirements such as accurate determination of prayer times, sightings of the moon, directions of the *qibla* and of Mecca, quantitative application of Muslim inheritance laws, and so forth. But in the age of the globalised positioning system, atomic clocks, and computers, it is difficult to point to religious imperatives for scientific progress.

If Muslim societies are to escape their ice age then they must accept modernity – which should not be confused with Westernisation – as desirable, and welcome the role of science, reason, and universal principles of law and justice in the arbitration of human affairs. Scarcity of material resources is not the primary issue and cannot be used as an excuse for arrested development. It will be crucial to allow dogmas to be challenged without incurring the charges of heresy and blasphemy. Muslims must understand that there is no alternative now to respecting personal freedom of thought, encouraging artistic and scientific creativity, cultivating a compulsive urge to innovate and experiment, and making education a vehicle of change.

Trusting scientists
Daniel Glaser

As a young PhD student in the early 1990s, studying vision by doing animal experimentation, I felt an understandable reluctance to engage with the general public on issues of ethics in science. In such work, the ivory tower still has steel-reinforced gates and 24-hour security. As I find myself now in 2004 working on similar questions but using human subjects (ballet dancers mostly), the idea of interacting with non-scientists about my work is much more inviting. But as well as moving on in my own professional circumstances, there have been several notable trends in the application of ethics to science and its relation to public engagement that are changing the terrain through which the individual scientist must navigate.

Ethics is often seen as the professional realm of philosophers and the practical realm of politicians and the judiciary. Various restricted strategies are employed to embed some ethical discourse into an otherwise rarefied biomedical context. But they are often piecemeal and disconnected. For example, some hospitals now have professional ethicists who can be 'bleeped' in an ethical emergency. To the extent that the law deals with ethics it can inform medical decisions, although this may result in a rather stunted 'defensive' medicine. Consideration of intellectual property rights and, more recently, equal opportunities employment law are gradually penetrating academia, spearheaded by those fields with clear commercial exploitability. In a more constructive sense, many medical and some scientific degrees now incorporate some ethical course units, although they are often free-standing and not integrated with the everyday practice of research (almost like moral first-aid training).

But why should the active scientist develop a position on ethics in a public context? That scientific research generates ethical issues has been clear since Archimedes at least. The pure scientist leaping naked from his bath was also the architect of fearsome engines of naval warfare. But since it is the generals who launch the weapons of war, scientists have been able to argue that they have no special responsibility for the applications of their discoveries. Often this is achieved by attempting to distinguish their work from that of a technologist, with science covering the discovery, and technology its application. At best, it is claimed, scientists are more informed than a lay person, but their ethical judgments are not privileged. Scientists have been portrayed as being as ethically disenfranchised as any other public group in modern society.

The least worst option so far
How is the scientist's voice privileged and in what kind of context can it be given legitimacy? One aspect that is central to the identity of scientific discourse is peer review. This is the primary mode of written scientific interaction, although a recent working party on equipping the public with an understanding of peer review (*www.senseaboutscience.org*) has pointed out that few non-scientists understand the process.

The peer-reviewed literature comprises a set of journals usually published weekly or monthly. Some journals cover high profile results from any scientific area *(Science* magazine or *Nature),* while others are aimed at increasingly specialised scientific audiences within a specific field *(The Journal of Sub-Cellular Fluorescence Spectroscopy).* All publish only scientific work that has undergone a specific selection process. Upon submission, the editor, usually an expert in the domain, sends the paper for review by a number of suitably qualified peer scientists. While the author's identity is known to the reviewers, the reviewers generally remain anonymous. A favourite game among authors is to try and guess the identity of the anonymous reviewers. Conversely, demanding that the author cite your work is one of the surest ways to blow your cover as a reviewer. Based on the reviewers' comments, the editor will either decide to accept the paper as is, require that the authors revise the paper to satisfy the reviewers' criticisms; or reject it outright.

This process has obvious practical and ethical flaws. As the author Nigel Calder has recently pointed out, it inherently produces scientific conservatism. Given that most scientific funding is also allocated by peer review, progress tends to take place in areas that established scientists already agree are significant. Maverick science is almost impossible to pursue under this kind of regime. It is a commonplace among historians of science that most scientific revolutionaries (for example Galileo) were wrong, given the evidence available at the time. Conversely, however, most people whose work goes against all the available evidence are also usually wrong. Science cannot tolerate too many revolutions and still hope to claim authority and be relied upon for solutions to practical problems. But encouraging a proper amount of risk-taking is also vital for a healthy scientific climate. This problem has not been examined sufficiently, and yet it constructs scientific culture at its most fundamental.

Peer review also generates more than its fair share of ethical issues. Every working scientist can give examples of work that has not been published because of personal dislikes, or scientific errors that have been propagated through political pressure. Peer review is considered the 'least worst' option, but little explicit ethical training is provided to help the average scientist find his or her feet. Interestingly, equal opportunities legislation is beginning to penetrate previously unilluminated areas of scientific practice such as hiring and promotion. It is the human resources departments of universities that are forcing scientists to examine and document their prejudices and practices, and are meeting with stiff resistance. However, the data protection act gives individuals the right to see almost anything that is written about them, and sex and race discrimination laws put the burden of proof on to the person making the decision. Even today many postdoctoral research positions are offered in the corridors at conferences, but on current trends this will rapidly become untenable. It may be that the mechanisms of anonymous peer review will be open to similar challenges in the near future. This may result in a fairer system, or may make the whole process unworkable.

Despite these problems, peer review still brings a sense of validation or even sanctification to the scientist's output, and preserves the sense that scientific stories can be removed from actual questions of policy or even pragmatic decisions. As an aside, this is why some people have called for there to be more MD/PhD programmes, to bring practical science closer to clinical practice. Of course the scientists whose job it is to consider practical problems are often those who work for governments or private corporations, such as oil and pharmaceutical companies. Unfortunately a 2002 MORI poll conducted for the Scientific Alliance has shown these to be the scientists trusted least by the public. Efforts to address public concerns must determine whether measures employing the scientists who actually work in these areas will increase public trust or public scepticism. It is clear that different pressures pertain to public and private science: that is, research taking place taking place in academic compared with commercial locations. The same peer review publication model is applied in both cases, although corrective mechanisms are increasingly applied to address explicit conflicts of interest. Of course, as universities become more tuned to the exploitability of discoveries, these interests become more and more commonly conflicting.

MMR: case study

Relying on scientists to report their own conflicts of interest can create problems. The recent debate about the MMR (measles/mumps/rubella) vaccine and its possible side effects is a case in point. Much of the controversy about a possible link between MMR and autism was sparked by a paper in *The Lancet* in 1998. It turned out some years later, partly as a result of journalistic investigation, that the lead author had several conflicts of interest that could plausibly have affected the core findings. In response, the journal editor wrote that he would never have accepted the paper had he known then what is now known. The conflict was not only about motivation for the study, but in fact methodological, involving selection of subjects, and could have had an effect on the statistics central to the claim of the paper.

Another extreme, and potentially more systematic, problem has recently been described in the press. In a much more cynical abuse, it is alleged that clinicians have been presented by drug companies with a 'finished' report of the efficacy of a drug, lacking only the name of the author. They are then invited to submit the report as their own work to high-profile journals. The prevalence of such practice is hard to verify since self-report is unlikely, and active deception implicit in such practice, but it highlights the vulnerability of the current system to any full-frontal assault with commercial (or even ideological) intent.

A further element of the MMR publication story concerns the distinction between peer-reviewed work and the discourse that exists in the penumbra that surrounds it. In the MMR story it was statements made in the press conference called to publicise the paper that gave rise to much public disquiet and anxiety. By contrast, the eminent science journalist Rita Carter has said that she never bases her research on interviews or informal discussions with scientists – why should their speculations be any more valid as base material than those of anyone else? Instead she always begins with the peer-reviewed literature and then interviews the scientists for clarification and illustration. The press releases that accompany a potentially high-profile paper are not of course peer reviewed, since they are outside the scientific discourse itself. While lay language summaries and clarifications are essential if a non-professional audience or readership is to understand a peer-reviewed story, there is a danger of oversimplification and plain misstatement, especially when scientists have not received media training. This is before anyone has even raised the question of the scientific literacy of journalists. While scientists readily complain about being misquoted, one press officer I have spoken to suggests that it is often a case of imperfect recollection by the scientist. There is a clear difference in knowledge and training between professional science journalists and news or even political correspondents, although of course the most important and contentious questions will often end up being covered by the least scientifically qualified.

Press releases frequently become contentious when universities collaborate with drug companies, usually through their funding of research projects. Government statements have recently identified this as an area where British science must improve. In such cases, tensions are frequently exposed. A principled university press officer can find him- or herself at the sharp end of such contradictions. As results emerge through conference proceedings and papers submitted but not yet accepted, pressure to announce new findings can mount. Again, 'relevance' here may have a damaging effect: it will be far easier for a canny PR company to pitch a result that will impinge on a large patient group or common disorder. And it can be argued that journalists, especially non-science journalists, may not be sensitive to the nuances of conference abstracts, reviewed or not, and may therefore take the lay summary of a peer-reviewed result to have the same status as the result itself. For example, the leading science journal *Nature* has very clear guidelines on press embargoes. The key is to encourage free scientific interactions at scientific conferences where press and public may incidentally be present, but to forbid the active courting of publicity prior to peer-review publication. Nevertheless, despite their threat of tough sanctions, the need for detailed guidelines reveals again the extent to which such codes rely on gentlemanly conduct on the part of the scientist.

Papers being peer reviewed almost always have more than one author. The integration of individual voices into an undifferentiated collective often causes further problems. This was revealed again in the MMR story, where a growing number of the authors of the initial paper have distanced themselves from the consequences (direct or otherwise) of its publication. Such disintegrations of group responsibility are surprisingly rare, given the extremely complicated and traumatic process that precedes the determination of the final list of authors and their order. There can be few more striking examples of the disconnection between the scientific and the public view of science than this pivotal moment. Even within science the issue must be considered arcane. The question of who is an author is not simply a question of who did the work. In some cases, having secured the funding is a sufficient criterion for authorship even when no further intellectual input is even suggested. In others, the one who did the actual work may be dropped for political reasons. In some fields such as physics papers are often published with dozens of authors. Single author papers are comparatively rare. One golden rule of science is that authorship should be decided at the beginning of the project, but as projects develop, relative contributions change, and disputes often arise. Once the list is fixed, the status accorded even depends on your position on the list. Confusingly, the high-status position varies depending on the scientific area. In some fields, alphabetical order rules; in others first author is junior, last is senior and the rest fight it out. These peculiar rites are more than quaint, since they serve to invest the moment of publication with an almost mystical quality and therefore to insulate the scientist from a reading of his or her work that is more publicly nuanced.

Over the last couple of years, the conventional model of peer-reviewed journals generally run for profit by commercial publishers, has been challenged by open-access models, in which the author pays. The rhetorical attack that has accompanied this suggests that universities are being held to ransom, with their libraries forced to 'buy back' from publishers the fruits of research work that has been paid for by the university in the first place. This is not only considered unfair by the big universities, but has a more serious consequence: poorer institutions, especially, but not exclusively, in developing countries, cannot afford access at all.

Critically, it also means that peer-reviewed papers are not available to the general public, and therefore attempts to encourage non-scientists to become informed and engaged in this discourse are effectively stymied. Two major initiatives have been launched to combat this structure: by the Public Library of Science (PLoS), in America, which is 'a non-profit organisation of scientists and physicians committed to making the world's scientific and medical literature a freely available public resource' and by BioMed Central, in Europe. In both cases article-processing charges are payable upon submission and many research funders automatically agree to pay this. The final journal article is available online, free to anyone, and copyright can rest with the author.

Currently only one per cent of the published literature is open access, and the big publishers are fighting back. While some concede that they have been greedy in the past, they argue that their impartial role outside the academy is a lynchpin and guarantee of good practice in the peer-review process, and adds value, which must be paid for. They claim that the public-access model would surrender control of the literature to coterie groups with vested scientific interests as outlined earlier, and that the model is economically unsustainable for small-scale specialist journals. Some publishers are trying partial models, such as making older articles freely available. Given the mixture of ideology and big corporate profits, the arguments are heated and sometimes bitter, and it remains to be seen what the effect will be in practice over the next year or two. Certainly the lofty ideals and practical proposals of the open-access movement align with many of the tenets of enlightened public engagement. This link should be strengthened.

Translating results into advice

When scientific results need to be translated into real-world recommendations, often the composition of groups becomes more fragile. A recent striking example relates to the efficacy or indeed harm of screening for early signs of breast cancer across various population groups. Controversy followed a review of the evidence issued by the well-respected Cochrane Group Inc. The methodology they employed was a meta-analysis, taking as a group all previous research and trying to resolve statistically significant patterns from the collective body that were not discernible from each alone. Unsurprisingly perhaps, the dispute centred on which studies should be excluded from the meta-analysis due to methodological flaws. If it turned out that most of the 'flawed' studies tended to have results in a certain direction, the pruning can change the bottom line. Such pruning is a notorious feature of scientific practice, most famously illustrated in Robert Millikan's 1909 oil-drop experiment looking for a quantum (smallest indivisible) electrical charge. Not all his data were included in the final publication, and his lab book famously contains remarks such as: 'Exactly right', 'Publish this Beautiful one', 'Error high will not use', 'Perfect Publish', 'Won't work'. More subtly, most scientists more often check their apparatus or analysis method when they get a result they do not expect.

Of course review articles make judgments about the relative validity of various peer-reviewed works, but here, where the work must be translated into practical consequences, the stakes (and desire of individuals to be accountable) are higher. A group convened under the auspices of the American environment protection agency to report on safe levels of pesticide exposure for children found that it was unable to agree a conclusion. Several members resigned towards the end of the process and issued a 'minority report' whose conclusions were diametrically opposed to those contained within the official version. This failure of consensus reveals how the need to provide practical answers to an emotive and safety-critical question can strain the normal processes of academic review.

The issue of screening is particularly challenging because of the emotive nature of this disease, the considerable need for proper education in order for a campaign to be effective, and the counter-intuitive nature of some of the debates. In particular, it is hard to appreciate why all possible investigations should not be tried on everyone when the consequences of missing a cancer are so catastrophic. The arguments consider the possible negative effects of the investigation (including some evidence that biopsies promote the growth of new blood vessels that can trigger the growth of a tumour), and the fact that many 'pre-cancerous' cells may never develop further (the old adage that men die either *of* prostate cancer or *with* prostate cancer). Of course research and treatment are not independent, since no statistics on the longitudinal time course of such test results, if left untreated, can be gathered under certain treatment policies.

Are there models outside science which can be exploited? The rise of 'evidence-based medicine' provokes the obvious question 'so what were they basing it on before?', but also attests to the need for formal strategies for translating a scientific approach into findings that can be implemented. It is interesting that this movement is driven more from the medical side: is evidence-based medicine more fashionable than patient-directed science? My own work takes place in a basic research institute, which is across the square from a neurological hospital. On sunny days patients undergoing rehabilitation are often wheeled into the park, and it is sometimes hard not to feel guilty that my research is not more directed towards curing disease. Of course blue-skies research has always led indirectly to medical progress, but for an individual's work to be effective the key lies in personal motivation.

Yet the thresholds applied to what counts as a significant result must differ when they may be used to address practical questions. Many researchers in pure science would be horrified if their results were applied unmediated to clinical questions, whether at a policy or individual case level. Certainly the kinds of thinking required for medical studies are quite different from those for pure science research. Indeed, despite the desirability of such amalgamated courses, individual students often find it necessary to divide their time between the two aspects carefully, to allow them sufficient time to switch mindsets.

But there is one sphere where science may indeed be able to learn from medical trends, and that is in the implementation of ethics. Medical ethics is a relatively well-established field of research, and the image of the white-coated philosopher sprinting down the hospital corridor to answer an emergency bleep is not too far-fetched. The beginnings of a willingness to allow other disciplines to have a say in day-to-day practice is not simply the result of increasingly litigious patients. It reflects a more general approach to informed consent and shared decision-making between doctors and patients, facilitated in many cases by philosophical statements of the issues at hand. However, it is only in the last year or two that a parallel movement of 'scientific ethics' is coming about. Recently, groups like Ethox – The Oxford Centre for Ethics and Communication in Health Care – have started to examine whether the interdisciplinary insights gained from medical ethics might be relevant to science, particularly its practical applications. This opening up does present challenges, since ethics strives for an isotropic perspective on practical questions: one which does not depend on your individual interests but is optimal when considered simultaneously from all sides. Such discourse is undermined by the prevalence of detached scientists, expressing their thoughts to one another in obscure language, and following an intellectual agenda which is publicly funded but directed only by discussion with their peers.

Of course it is not just philosophers among non-scientists who might have a privileged role. It can even be asked whether a scientific training is a proper preparation for making practical determinations. Five of the six authors we shortlisted for this year's Aventis Prize for Science Books are professional writers rather than active research scientists. All had consulted extensively with scientists, but one might infer that presentation is more important than knowledge or practical experience of research in presenting an engaging and accessible scientific story. Perhaps, by this token, it is civil servants, lawyers or even politicians who should be responsible for drawing up consensus views on scientific questions.

Clearly top-level funding decisions about state-sponsored science do fall within more general political spending considerations. Here, scientists lobby like any other special interest group, selling the importance of the scientific sector and of their own area within it. Of course, increased scientific literacy among politicians and civil servants would enhance the likelihood of reasonable decisions, but equally, public understanding of science must increase if there is to be a meaningful democratic engagement at the level of funding priorities.

In public discourse, scientific questions tend to be put under an ethical spotlight in a small set of 'issues' which evolve from year to year and from country to country. In the UK today obvious examples include the MMR vaccine and its possible link with autism, the siting of mobile phone masts, GM crops and foods, and questions surrounding human fertility, reproduction and cloning.

The focus on polarised issues generates specific problems. First, since they are newsworthy they are generally covered in the press and media by news and features journalists rather than the skilled and generally very professional science correspondents. This often results in the effective but emotive communication of restricted aspects of a question, and can rapidly generate intuitively compelling imagery that is impossible to modify (Frankenstein foods; the dangers of railway travel). These issues can spawn activist groups some of which promote a frankly anti-scientific agenda, which in turn can generate a symmetrically closed response from elements of the scientific community. The escalating cycle of mistrust which sometimes results is extremely difficult to combat.

With such entrenched arguments, public engagement is often too late. For example, recent work to promote informed public debate about genetically modified food in the UK had a worrying outcome. It has been a theoretical commonplace in science communication that public understanding of science is not the same as public acceptance of science, but in the GM case it was found that the more exposure people had to scientific information the more opposed they became. This may confirm suspicions that efforts to direct new scientific research and public engagement activity towards issues where public alarm has been generated are often doomed, since many will automatically disbelieve a conclusion that does not support their entrenched position. Interestingly, efforts to bring together different sides to discuss these questions succeed best when role playing is employed to generate discussion of fictitious or unrelated scientific scenarios. As John Durant of the At-Bristol Science Centre has pointed out, there are three kinds of scientific knowledge that might enlighten the public: scientific facts, how science works, and how science *really* works. Scientific facts or stories are self-explanatory. 'How science works' might refer to the development of experiments to test hypotheses and the use of statistics, and is important in showing, for example, that science can never prove that something is completely safe, but only fail to find dangers. 'How science *really* works' deals with conflicts of interest and the other kinds of ethical issues raised above.

Cafés Scientifiques

How can public ignorance, especially on 'How science really works', be combated? Of course the media, education – both general and scientific, the structure of scientific discourse, including peer review and the politics behind science and science funding, can all be improved. But I would like to emphasise a particular approach that harnesses a bottom-up process, not one restricted to a small number of popularisers, or lay members of ethics committees. What is required is an extensive social interpenetration, allowing scientific practice to escape from the laboratory and the library and engage a broad and curious public.

At the Institute of Contemporary Arts, I chair a London version of Café Scientifique. This is one particular practical attempt to promote local, regular interactions between scientists and non-scientists, which is derived from the French Café Philosophique, and was developed by a television producer from Leeds named Duncan Dallas. It is a non-hierarchical and democratic formula for involving non-scientists in a scientific discussion, and is held in a café or other informally seated setting, ideally outside an academic institution, often with an experienced facilitator. A speaker talks for 20 minutes or so and gives an outline of his or her field and a couple of relevant questions, generally without slides or visual aids. There is then a ten-minute break for informal discussion and refilling of drinks. This pause combats the 'thinking of a question on the bus on the way home' phenomenon, allowing individuals and small groups to formulate and mutually validate their responses. There is then a discussion, typically just under an hour, involving – but not led – by the speaker. It is not a question and answer session, and the expert's voice does not dominate. Paradoxically, it is often the silent presence of a professional that legitimates and promotes an empowered discussion.

The idea is to generate community-based structures in a non-professional context, where the public can discuss scientific issues with experts. These are not lectures or demonstrations. Since they are not primarily about contentious issues, they escape from many of the problems outlined earlier. By weakening the conventional power relationships and specialist language that conversations in a scientific institution involve, they encourage individual non-scientists to develop their own scientific questions and opinions. An appreciation of the practice of science weakens common misconceptions, such as the assumption that a dissenting scientific voice necessarily means that a field is fatally split. These insights are not conveyed didactically, but arise naturally from a new familiarity with the everyday life of science

Cafés can take many different forms. On a recent British Council tour, I chaired three on climate change in three towns in three days, with the writer and campaigner Mark Lynas. In a literary café in Berne, an urbane mixture of diplomats, scientists and other local intelligentsia considered the intersection of the personal and the political. We savoured the irony inherent in the fact that 90 per cent of them believed something should be done about global warming, but 90 per cent had flown in the last 12 months. In rural Altdorf, the café was half in German and half in English. Local mountaineers related their own experiences of melting permafrost and discussed whether a small community could make a global difference, concluding that small-scale, symbolic actions could be effective. Finally, in Davos, a sceptical audience at an avalanche research institute grilled Mark on his selective use of evidence. Local businessmen and journalists argued that scientific credibility needed to be balanced against effective communication, and that dramatic examples do inspire action. In all three cases, more than half of the 50 people present spoke and the discussion continued informally for over an hour afterwards. While the issues were important (saving the planet and so forth) what was inspiring was to see a free-flowing conversation involving experts and non-experts equally. This was public engagement in process and content.

Excitingly, many of these issues of trust and public involvement are relevant in a more general political and social context. For example, the recent Apeldoorn Dutch–English binational conference concentrated on the challenge of 'narrowing the gap between the political class and the public at national and European levels'. As a British Council-invited speaker, I described the Café Scientifique in this context and, in its structure and successful uptake, it appeared to offer a practical tool to address many of the issues of empowerment and alienation that have been identified in all sorts of spheres. The undeniable fascination that scientific stories generate among non-experts of all ages makes these kinds of scientific engagement an attractive model for more general grass-roots, non-hierarchical democratic activity. But, the structure has the power to undermine hierarchical knowledge tyrannies of all sorts. As more scientists gain the courage and experience that enables them to engage directly in this kind of publicly validated ethical practice, the scientific domain may come to be seen as a leading example of this kind of transformation, and other areas of expertise, other concentrations of power, remote from engaged public scrutiny, will come to seem more and more anomalous.

The way we trust now: the authority of science and the character of the scientists

Steven Shapin

Many scientists are seriously concerned about what they take to be a crisis in public confidence. For example, Hugh Grant – zoologist and CEO of Monsanto – who told the *Financial Times* this June that we're rapidly moving from a 'trust me' society to a 'show me' society:

> 'A "trust me" society is a paternalistic society that says, "don't worry about it, it'll be fine, I know best, we have your interests at heart, this will work". The "show me" society says, "I might not understand the data – and that's OK if I don't – but I want to know that I can access it at any time, and I want to know that my views are relevant to this debate".'

Monsanto had to take into account both the reality and the consequences of this shift in sentiment, not least because, as Grant said, they'd 'bet the company' on the success of genetically modified foods, and the public wasn't swallowing them as the company, its scientists, and its shareholders would like.

Grant's views are familiar. It is not hard to find any number of similar expressions from leading scientists, especially, but not exclusively, in biomedicine, biotech, molecular biology, nanotechnology, and in energy companies. The public, it is said, has grown sceptical, sour, and unappreciative; scientists are subject to more vigorous surveillance than they have been used to; and their disinterestedness is no longer taken for granted.

Whether the issue is fraud or commercial bias, scientists have grown uneasily accustomed to both internal and governmental instruments checking their work to make sure it is on the level. Grant's conclusion was just that scientists had better get used to these fundamentally new circumstances, do their best to explain themselves, and open up the house of science to public inspection. Such sentiments are linked to a widespread condemnation of the 'public misunderstanding of science': if the public knew more science, it is often asserted, they'd trust scientists more. In any case, and with whatever consequences, Grant's strong formulation of the decline of a trust society surrounding science is widely shared.

Widely, but not universally. Writing a few months before in *The New York Review of Books,* Richard Horton, editor of *The Lancet,* responded to the same public concerns about the 'corruption of science' that were to occupy Grant. But, for Horton, the 'escalating corrosion of values' in biomedical science is a reality. It derives from structural changes that occurred in the 1970s and early 1980s in the commercial relations of academic science and, more fundamentally, in the commercial possibilities of science. The public and its representatives are indeed worried about the effects of these changes on the integrity of science, but scientists themselves, Horton thinks, ought to be more worried, as they have fouled their own nest.

However, Horton differs from Grant in two interesting respects. First, he does not accept that a 'trust society' has been wholly dissolved, or, more interestingly, that it even could be so dissolved. We might say that trust has been compromised, but cannot intelligibly say that a trust society has been replaced by a surveillance society. If there were no trust in scientists, you would not get more reliable scientific knowledge; you would get no knowledge at all. For Horton, this means that the integrity of scientists is fundamental: it cannot either be improved or replaced by an apparatus of control. Remove grounds for believing that scientists hold themselves to a different moral order and you really will dissolve scientific knowledge and whatever public authority it might have. Even if, Horton writes, 'personal virtue has indeed given way to impersonal expertise, and if moral character has become secondary to institutional prestige, it would be wrong to conclude that the connection between public trust and the integrity of the individual scientist has been wholly erased'. Nor could it be.

Second, Horton does something rare for a scientist or physician in these connections: he seeks to comprehend the way we live now and to appreciate present risks and opportunities by learning something from history. I should immediately declare an interest here, since the history Horton turns to is mine – specifically a book I wrote ten years ago on the relationship between ideas of gentlemanly honour and intellectual authority in 17th century England.[1] Horton uses history to orientate us to long-standing problems in the relations between commercial concerns for property and scientific imperatives towards openness: '[Shapin] argues that our personal knowledge of the world depends to a large degree on what others tell us. Our understanding therefore has a moral character, based as it must be on trust. In constructing a body of reliable individual knowledge, trustworthy people are crucial. Secret scientific knowledge and commercial exploitation of discoveries thus have a long and much-abhorred history within science, whatever scientists might claim in order to justify themselves today.'

I want to repay Horton's constructive use of history by telling him some more history that he, other concerned scientists, policy-makers, and lay people might find interesting. If the imputed integrity of scientists really is central to the authority of scientific knowledge, then how and why did our culture apparently give up the idea that scientists were morally different from anyone else? Get some kind of grip on the history of this cultural change, and perhaps – as in the case of public trust in science – we can better understand our current predicament, what brought it into being, what sustains it, and what possibilities there might therefore be for change. In particular, I want to suggest that the shift from Grant's 'trust me society' to a 'show me society' is, and can only be, partial. There are matters of principle here, and it is necessary to start by giving some account of them.

The necessity of trust

In what does the public authority of scientists consist? An obvious answer is that authority flows from expertise. Who knows more about heredity than a geneticist, more about rocks than a geologist, more about how your heart works than a cardiologist? Knowing more is associated with power to do more, and, even if the public care little about the scope and depth of knowledge – that's not their business – they surely care quite a lot about technique and the capacity effectively to intervene in the course of nature. Who would trust a car mechanic to fix their heart, a cardiologist to fix their car, or a well-meaning friend ignorant of both hearts and cars to fix either? Power to act is seen to derive from the scope and quality of expert knowledge. So technical expertise is central to questions about the authority of knowledge and 'knowers' in our sort of society. There is no getting around the fact.

Yet there is some difference between expertise as a feature of technical authority and as a sufficient response to questions about authority. I want, first, to be clear about what is meant by the authority of scientific expertise; second, to point out some problems attending distinctions between technical expertise and moral authority; problems associated with Grant's description of ours as a 'show me society'. Finally, I trace some moments in the historical trajectory that have produced present-day thinking about the technical and the moral, and remark on some practical difficulties that flow from that way of thinking.

There are at least three problems involved in the notion that technical expertise offers an adequate basis for public trust. To start with, expertise cannot be known directly. Trust in expertise depends first upon locating that expertise. If you know yourself to be an expert in some domain, then there is no problem for you: you are satisfied on quite direct grounds, even though you may be wrong. But in such cases there is little interest in saying that one 'trusts oneself'. In the nature of things, and for our sort of society, expertise is almost always external: it belongs to someone else and our problem is how to recognise it, access it, and mobilise it. The rationalist, individualist tradition our culture inherits from the 17th-century philosopher John Locke insists that proper knowledge is knowledge whose warrants are wholly within one's own compass: we only really know what we see at first-hand or what we can prove with our own minds.

Yet the practical consequence of embracing such individualism should be the recognition that we have scarcely any proper knowledge at all. Instead, almost all of our stock of knowledge – I would like to say all, but that would take more time to argue – is held by courtesy, through reliance on others, on the basis of authority and trust. I know that *this* particular cardiologist is an expert because I read it several months ago in *Boston Magazine*'s article on 'good doctors', and I know that credentialled cardiologists are the sort of people to go to if I've got heart problems, on the basis of a diffuse range of trusted sources, from school teachers to colleagues to printed and digital media to direct contact with general practitioners. Despite widespread current unease about a climate of mistrust in authenticated experts, the fact of the matter is that no society has ever reposed as much trust as ours in the power of expertise. That is one reason for the widespread rhetorical identification of scientists with priests or magicians. The present-day problem is not mistrust in scientists but, rather, a problem in deciding who the scientific experts really are.

It is important to avoid the tendency to think of the laity as 'other people'. Even experts are lay people with respect to the technical knowledge that lives, so to speak, next door: physicians heal themselves just on the condition that they are the right sort of specialists. Hence, in proper usage, the notion of the laity should not be used to pick out 'them versus us', taken as stable social categories; it is not a discriminator like 'working class'. Recognition of expertise one can safely rely upon depends on a prior ability to trust those that testify to where expertise lives. In our society, people come to radically different conclusions about these things; why else would we have so many people on the Atkins Diet when the American Heart Association and the USDA Food Guide Pyramid counsel so strongly against 'low-carb, high-fat' diets?

The second problem flows from this: in late modern society, technical expertise tends to speak with different voices, increasingly so as expertise extends its reach into more and more areas of political, economic, and personal concern. Psychiatric expert witnesses war with each other in court; geologists are at odds over the long-term safety of storage sites for radioactive waste; biologists disagree in public over how much mercury your body can safely carry; and, of course, you can pick whatever expert-endorsed regime you like when it comes to raising your children, being irresistible to the opposite (or same) sex, or losing weight. These things are not trivial. A very high degree of expert consensus does indeed mark the natural sciences, but only on the condition that you equate science with its textbook and classroom incarnations. The puzzle-solving, precision-seeking, domain-extending phenomena of Thomas Kuhn's 'normal science' are very real.

However, expert disagreement is both endemic and consequential in just those areas where political decisions about what we should do are involved. Whether twice two equals four, or whether DNA is the genetic substance, is not currently in the political domain. But what should be done with radioactive waste, and what is the correct diet for safe weight loss, very much are. Expert disagreement is to be regarded not as a marginal, trivial, and transient problem – 'the truth will out in the end' – but as constitutive of science when it figures in political decision-making processes, where we always have to decide what to do before 'the truth comes out', before knowledge consolidates enough to put in a textbook and test children on it. You might just as reasonably say that 'the essence of science is disagreement' as stress the defining role of consensus. It depends upon the scientific arena you look at. It follows from expert disagreement that trusting experts necessitates a decision about *which* experts to trust. When the expert community itself hasn't come to any settled view about the identity of genuine expertise, it is asking a lot to expect the public to do so.

Third, there is a point of principle involved in the move from knowing more – which is a technical matter – to doing the right thing – which is a moral and political matter. As the American biologist David Starr Jordan once said: 'Wisdom is knowing what to do next, skill is knowing how to do it, and virtue is doing it.' Technical expertise, that is to say, is a necessary but not a sufficient condition for effective action to achieve the ends you might wish and think to be good. The cardiologist has to care about *your* heart as well as to know a lot about hearts; the geologist has to be acting in the public interest, rather than trying to augment the bottom line of a property developer; the expert nutritionist has got to testify to what he or she believes to be the truth, rather than attending to the profits of the beef-packing industry.

So, in order for trust in experts to have its practical grip, we have to be satisfied not just that certain individuals know more but also that they are well-intentioned, and that, if we trust them, they will try their best to do the right thing, even if – just because they are human – they cannot always bring about the right result. At a practical level, the evaluation of expertise contains within it a moral evaluation. Who are the experts, whom we can trust, as such, to do good?

Is/ought and the authority of science

At one point in our culture, there was a robust response to that question. The scientist, or, in past usage, the 'natural philosopher', was not just someone who knew more, but someone who was better than the common run of humanity or of scholars. There were several reasons why this might be believed, but one derived from the object of scientific study: Nature conceived as God's Second Book, on a hermeneutic par with the Bible, was a very different thing to nature understood as a chance concatenation of atoms. The first had the capacity to uplift those who studied it; the second did not.

In 1775, the English Unitarian chemist Joseph Priestley wrote that: 'A Philosopher ought to be something greater, and better than another man.' If the man of science was not already virtuous when he came to science, then the 'contemplation of the works of God should give sublimity to his virtue, should expand his benevolence, extinguish every thing mean, base, and selfish in [his] nature'. If we find such sentiments ridiculous today, it is in part because our view of natural reality has changed, courtesy of the consensual views of scientists themselves. The secularised object of their studies now contains no moral lessons and has no capacity for moral uplift. In 1898, Leo Tolstoy's essay on modern science described 'a strange misunderstanding' that lay at the heart of modern culture:

'A plain reasonable working man supposes, in the old way which is also the common-sense way, that if there are people who spend their lives in study, whom he feeds and keeps while they think for him – then no doubt these men are engaged in studying things men need to know; and he expects science to solve for him the questions on which his welfare and that of all men depends. He expects science to tell him how he ought to live: how to treat his family, his neighbours and the men of other tribes, how to restrain his passions, what to believe in and what not to believe in, and much else. But what does our science say to him on these matters? It triumphantly tells him how many million miles it is from the earth to the sun. "But I don't want any of those things", says a plain and reasonable man – "I want to know how to live".'

To which the modern scientist responds, in effect, 'that's not my business'.

This response is entirely reasonable from a modern point of view, and, in the view of many, it is a necessary condition for the objectivity and integrity of science. Science, to *be* science, cannot deal with the intractable and irredeemably subjective 'ought' but exclusively with the potentially consensual and objective 'is'; with fact and not with value. This self-denying ordnance made science powerful, but at the risk of moral irrelevance.

Nevertheless, it was a price that had to be paid. At any rate, this was the opinion of the sociologist Max Weber in his influential 1918 address, *Science as a Vocation*. The world was now, thanks to the scientists, 'disenchanted': 'there are no mysterious incalculable forces that come into play, but rather . . . one can, in principle, master all things by calculation'. Science once promised that it would show 'the path to God', the road to happiness or to virtue, but 'Who – aside from certain big children who are indeed found in the natural sciences – still believes that the findings of astronomy, biology, physics, or chemistry could teach us anything about the meaning of the world?'

During the late 19th-and early 20th century, the technical experts of Western society reflectively and systematically disengaged their work from the moral domain. The object of their study did not invite moralising, and the conditions of internal consensus and external credibility made forays from 'is' to 'ought' fraught with risk. Any slippage from the descriptive to the normative was not just the 'naturalistic fallacy' marked by philosophers from David Hume to G. E.

Moore; it was also ontologically unsustainable and politically inadvisable. If such people as 'moral experts' in modern society existed, they were not to be found in the laboratory or speaking from a scientific podium. This was, for example, Albert Einstein's opinion: 'knowledge of what is does not open the door directly to what *should be*':

> '[All] scientific statements and laws have one characteristic in common: they are "true or false" (adequate or inadequate). Roughly speaking, our reaction to them is "yes" or "no". The scientific way of thinking has a further characteristic. The concepts which it uses to build up its coherent systems are not expressing emotions. For the scientist, there is only "being," but no wishing, no valuing, no good, no evil; no goal. As long as we remain within the realm of science proper, we can never meet with a sentence of the type: "Thou shalt not lie." There is something like a Puritan's restraint in the scientist who seeks truth: he keeps away from everything voluntaristic or emotional.'

From calling to job

By the 1930s, professionalism and secularism had begun to characterise both the way in which scientists presented themselves to the world, and the way their work was understood by academic outsiders. Science was becoming a decently paid and well-regarded, but still ordinary, job, rather than a 'calling'. Scientists working in bureaucratised settings, those engaged in the making of profit and secular power especially, could no longer appear as wholly pure, and might even now worry about maintaining a disengaged image. Although much mid-century academic commentary seems not to have noticed, the vast majority of American scientists were not then employed in institutions of higher education, doing pure research intended to advance knowledge for the sake of knowledge. The 1966 National Register counted 243,000 working scientists, with 37 per cent holding PhDs. Of these latter, only 36 per cent were employed in educational institutions, 34 per cent in industry and business, and 13 per cent by federal, state, and local governments. (In Britain, which was spending a far smaller proportion of its national income on industrial research than the USA, the crystallographer J. D. Bernal estimated in 1939 that 70 per cent of all qualified scientific workers were employed in industry.) Disinterestedness, and its associated virtues, is far easier to ascribe to the powerless than to the powerful, and, through their increasing association with business and the military after the Second World War, scientists were becoming increasingly familiar with the corridors of power.

In 1940, G. H. Hardy's bittersweet *A Mathematician's Apology* warned: 'We must guard against a fallacy common among apologists of science – the fallacy of supposing that the men whose work most benefits humanity are thinking much of that while they do it; that physiologists, for example, have particularly noble souls.' A few years later, insistence on the moral ordinariness of science was a keystone of Robert K. Merton's justification for a sociological approach. 'A passion for knowledge, idle curiosity, altruistic concern with the benefit to humanity, and a host of other special motives,' Merton wrote in 1942, 'have been attributed to the scientist. The quest for distinctive motives appears to have been misdirected.' There is, he said, 'no satisfactory evidence' that scientists are 'recruited from the ranks of those who exhibit an unusual degree of moral integrity' or that the objectivity of scientific knowledge proceeds from 'the personal qualities of scientists.' You could rightly defer to scientists' technical expertise, but there was no reason for deference in any area outside their special expertise, for example, on matters concerning 'what ought to be done'.

By the post-Second World War period, insistence on the moral ordinariness of the scientist had become an American cultural commonplace. In 1950, the point of Anthony Standen's *Science is a*

Sacred Cow was that science should not be treated as a sacred cow, just as Ralph Lapp's 1965 *The New Priesthood* warned against the dangerous mistake of treating scientists as priests. Lapp worried about what later came to be called 'technocracy', while Standen took for granted that the legend of heroic virtuosity persisted in some quarters, only to identify the myth-makers not with practicing scientists but with moralising educationists ('scientific evangelists') and warn the public against their credulity:

> '. . . we are having wool pulled over our eyes if we let ourselves be convinced that scientists, taken as a group, are anything special in the way of brains. They are very ordinary professional men, and all they know is their own trade, just like all other professional men.'

Nor are scientists better than anyone else at predicting an inherently unpredictable future, even when they forecast the future course of science and technology. Knowing more science never means knowing much, if anything, about its future trajectory.

In 1964, Jacques Barzun's *Science, The Glorious Entertainment* pointed to the loss of integrity and freedom associated with the scientist becoming the servant of the state and 'the darling of industry'. The old cosmopolitan loyalties to the free Republic of Science had been replaced by local loyalties to governments or to companies. In the same vein, the sociologist Joseph Schneider bearded the natural scientists in their own lair when he wrote in *The Scientific Monthly*: 'There was a time when men of mind expressed only contempt for the vainglorious show of politics and war. But today the man of science has become a hireling, a willing subject in the service of the nation state; an indefatigable combatant in the righteous cause of a finite warrior god.' And in 1968, Spencer Klaw's *The New Brahmins: Scientific Life in America,* observed, 'the patronage [that scientists now] command, has inevitably changed the nature of their calling. They have become richer and more caught up in worldly affairs,' as he recorded the older generation's dismay about the linked rise of hack-work and the decline of both genius and virtue.

Many scientists themselves very vigorously insisted on their collective moral ordinariness, warning the public, for that reason, against excessive trust in science. In 1963, the biochemist Erwin Chargaff composed a sour, modern dialogue in which an idealistic 'old chemist' (Chargaff himself) was lectured by a trendily ambitious 'young molecular biologist':

> 'You seem,' the young man sneered, 'to have the romantically foolish idea that only a good man can be a good scientist.' The 'old chemist' conceded the charge but not its foolishness: 'It is always dangerous to use the argument *ad hominem*, and you should not judge from yourself. But is it not a desperate situation when an old proverb must be reversed to read: Wherever the fish stinks there is its head?'

For the biologist Paul Weiss the rise of Big Science and the associated industrialisation of research were the decisive events compromising any notion of distinctive scientific integrity:

> 'Throughout the phase of history, which we have come to survey [the last three centuries], till very recently, to be a scientist was a calling, not a job. The scene, however, is now changing rapidly. The popularity and needs of an expanding science bring in more drifters and followers than pioneers. Shall we let brainpower be overgrown by manpower and mechanical rote performance?'

The appearance of James Watson's smash-hit account of the discovery of *The Double Helix* in 1968 was both an indicator and a further cause of these gathering shifts in sensibility: from the distance of over 35 years, it is not easy to recall the shock value of Watson's revelation that scientists might be motivated by the same sorts of concerns as anyone else.

Chargaff wrote that the belief that the scientific profession 'was a noble one . . . was certainly shattered in 1945', and, for the bomb-builders of the Manhattan Project, the stipulation of moral ordinariness had special significance. It was a way of laying the spectre of Dr Frankenstein: the idea that these appalling weapons had been brought into the world by bad men, badly motivated. Writing in 1960, C. P. Snow insisted upon moral equivalence as a way of showing the public that there was no reason to be 'frightened' of scientists, that scientists were 'certainly' not morally or temperamentally 'worse than other men.' J. Robert Oppenheimer, whose remark about physicists having come to 'know sin' was emblematic of a supposed collective descent from grace, recognised, but gently rejected, traditional views of the moral superiority of the scientist: 'The study of physics, and I think my colleagues in the other sciences will let me speak for them too, does not make philosopher–kings. It has not, until now, made kings. It almost never makes fit philosophers – so rarely that they must be counted as exceptions.' Just before his death, Oppenheimer drew a measured but sharp distinction between the vast technical knowledge that scientists possessed and the moral and political programmes of action in which scientific knowledge was increasingly enlisted:

'Among the things of which we cannot talk without some ambiguity, and in which the objective structure of the sciences will play what is often a very minor part, but sometimes an essential one, are many questions which are not private, which are common questions, and public ones: the arts, the good life, the good society. There is to my view no reason why we [scientists] should come to these with a greater consensus or a greater sense of valid relevant experience than any other profession. They need reason, and they need a preoccupation with consistency; but only in so far as the scientist's life has analogies with the artist's . . . only insofar as the scientist's life is in some way a good life, and his society a good society, have we any professional credentials to enter these discussions, and not primarily because of the objectivity of our communication and our knowledge.'

In the late 1960s, the physicist Ralph Lapp thought it important to tell the public that: 'Scientists as a group probably have no better sense of human values than any other group. To say that science seeks the truth does not endow scientists as a group with special wisdom of what is good for society. Furthermore, scientists have no single community within which there is a common set of values.' It followed from arguments like these that there would be no reason to pay any special attention to scientists' views on 'what should be done', certainly on matters that did not involve their particular expertise, and even when such decisions implicated technical expertise, which scientists alone possessed.

The advisory role of the scientists to the national security state represented a new form of technical power and authority, but the Oppenheimer security hearings of 1954, and later McCarthyite persecutions, soon offered dramatic lessons in the limits of that power. The state would continue to enlist scientific expertise, and to grant considerable autonomy and vast resources to those experts, but only on the condition that experts left whatever moral and political preferences they might have outside the doors to the corridors of power. Better yet, they should learn that they had no entitlement to expressions of special moral authority or political judgment. Should they insist on such authority, they risked losing access to the enormous material support that was being offered to scientists in the post-war decades. After the Oppenheimer hearings, the Board reminded the American scientific community of the boundaries that democratic society placed around technical expertise:

'A question can properly be raised about advice of specialists relating to moral, military and political issues, under circumstances which lend such advice an undue and in some cases decisive weight. Caution must be expressed with respect to judgments which go beyond areas of special and particular competence.'

Shortly afterwards, a commentator noted: 'They did not care what [Oppenheimer's] moral scruples were. It was the fact that he had any at all which was derogatory.' So the Board's *Final Report* announced: 'We know that scientists, with their unusual talents, are loyal citizens, and, for every pertinent purpose, normal human beings.' It was probably meant as a warning as much as a description. The 'is/ought' distinction, that is to say, was to be institutionalised in the modern scientific role as a condition of its political legitimacy. It was a contract that appealed to both parties: the political powers got expertise on-tap without interference in their prerogatives; the scientists got money and a reconfigured, but still worthwhile, version of autonomy.[2]

Problems of mistrust

If the transition from 'knowing more' to 'knowing what is the right thing to do' is understood as a move between distinct languages, and if our technical experts are considered to be no better than anyone else, then there is no basis for granting them any special moral authority. I have traced the historical development of just such beliefs, the result of which is a bias of technical experts to eschew debates over morality and policy, and of moralists and policy-makers to mistrust those technical experts who may still assert their special authority to make judgments about 'what ought to be done'. This state of affairs is increasingly taken as a matter of course in late modern society: how could it be otherwise?

Yet, for all the mutual convenience of the New Dispensation segregating technical expertise from moral authority, its legacy is a pervasive awkwardness in contemporary culture. This is particularly the case in debates about 'what ought to be done' in technoscientific matters bearing on public interests and preferences. Who has the right to speak and the authority to be listened to? It would be very foolish not to concede major rights and authority to relevant technical experts, especially insofar as the knowledge implicated in such decisions becomes more complex, arcane, and, ultimately, opaque to all but those few. Nor should such rights be limited by overblown fears of a 'technocratic' hegemony of experts, not least since the possibilities of such technocracy are limited by the varying voices with which expertise speaks in matters of public concern. Moreover, there are some seldom acknowledged problems attending the attributed moral ordinariness of technical experts, and it is to these problems I want finally to turn.

Scepticism is cheap to express, but often expensive in its consequences. If technical experts have no more moral rights to be trusted then anyone else, then it follows that two things must be done. First, we should design instruments of surveillance and control, designed to achieve what personal integrity is now supposed impotent to assure: government bureaus of research integrity, conflict of interest offices, requirements for declarations of financial interest in scientific journals, and, of course, informed consent regulations and institutional review boards. Given The Way We Live Now, it would be foolish not to implement such measures, and they would probably have at least some of the desired effects. But it would also be foolish to think that surveillance can ever be total, and, therefore, that the limitation of trust can ever approach the elimination of trust. Control and integrity must, for that reason, always work together, yet, as sociologists well understand, there is a tendency for people who are mistrusted to live down to expectations.

Second, if our experts are presumed to lack integrity and moral authority, we must put in place people specially trained to evaluate moral options and to advise on or make moral decisions. The rise of professional 'ethicists' and assorted moral experts is, indeed, a remarkable feature of recent times, and it is at once an expression of conviction in the moral ordinariness – or worse – of technical experts, and the withdrawal of trust in scientists and physicians to 'do the right thing'. But it is a delusion to suppose that morality can be simply and effectively offloaded to a cadre of experts. Even if one accepts the very idea of superior professional moral expertise – and I am not alone in finding that notion something between silly and disturbing – the problems of locating such moral expertise and trusting it are very much the same as those outlined in the case of technical expertise. How do you *recognise* genuine moral experts?

This objection is not pedantry: many bio- and medical ethics centres now depend massively upon funding from the pharmaceutical industry. In the USA, the further turn of the sceptical wheel began long ago.[3] *Quis custodiet ipsos custodes*? The regress is potentially infinite, and the economic, intellectual, and moral costs of travelling very far along that road are massive, crippling, and deeply disagreeable. Scepticism tends too easily to spread beyond the bounds within which one might like to keep it.

Late modern society has indeed travelled the sceptical road, but Richard Horton is right to remind Hugh Grant that it has not gone as far as the Monsanto CEO supposes. For an indicator of the extent to which a 'trust society' has not yet been dissolved, and to which technical experts are held to higher-than-ordinary standards of conduct, look no further than the extent to which both the public and many of our experts respond to occasions of scientists' materialism, malfeasance, corruption, and insensitivity with displays of shock and dismay. Again, as sociologists know very well, 'moral outrage' is a pretty good sign that an offence has been committed against what a society holds dear. The 'de-moralisation' of technical expertise is far from complete.

Since I have expressed doubts about the idea of external 'moral expertise', I can at once insist that I have no such credentials and excuse myself from telling scientists and their masters in any detail what they ought to do about the current malaise. Nevertheless, I am happy to underline what I think this story has to say to those whose concerns are more geared towards questions of 'what ought to be done'.

There is an almost inverse relationship between the ease of taking measures to cope with the de-moralisation of science and the likelihood that these measures will work. The current vogue for professionalising and calling upon ethical expertise is unlikely to be effective. It is relatively cheap; it gives the public an impression of 'doing something'; but solid evidence of its use is lacking. At the other extreme, if indeed the de-moralisation of science proceeds from such large-scale social and cultural changes as secularisation and professionalisation, the possibilities of positive action in these matters are slim to nil.

In pronouncing 'the disenchantment of nature' at the beginning of the 20th century, Max Weber described the conditions in which scientists could no longer be priests, moralists, or even morally uplifted by their work. Few present-day scientists would wish to unwind that bit of history, but no one can now be unconscious of the extent to which announcements of the Death of the Sacred were premature. Both Christian and Islamic fundamentalism have taken care of that. Neither is the 20th century professionalisation of the scientific career, and the transformation of science from a calling to a job, a change that anyone could undo, or that anyone who enjoys the fruits of Big Science-produced technology and medicine would wish to undo.

To return science to an avocation of the priest or the gentleman would be to change our society out of all recognition. Such a thing would be as undemocratic, unwise, and destructive to our current conceptions and expectations of science as it would be impossible to achieve. Late modern science *is* a job, increasingly sharing the characteristics and values of other professional and technical jobs. Our society has too many technoscientific problems in need of solution to advocate any significant shrinkage of the number of jobs available or the resources committed to the support of science.

But between the ineffectively easy and the impossibly visionary, there lie real opportunities for addressing current crises in scientific integrity and the consequent corrosive growth of public mistrust. One such possibility was pointed out in Horton's essay and is now being canvassed in various forms by many scientists and policy-makers. The commercialisation of science is pervasive, but science without large-scale commercial sponsorship or links is not inconceivable. Many areas of contemporary science continue to do their work totally or largely free of commercial subvention, and, even while academic scientists are continually pressed to make their research 'pay' and to seek out commercial sponsorship, governments – even now – accept some responsibility for picking up the tab for basic research when industry can't or won't. The building up of commercial ties delights governments and university administrators, but corporate executives and research managers have *never* uniformly taken the position that academia serves industry best by imitating industry. Since the beginnings of industrial research in the early 20th century, a number of thoughtful executives have urged universities to stick to their last, concentrating on those non-commercial lines of research that industry found it hard to justify and to execute.[4] In short, the scaling back of ties between commerce and academia is not inconceivable, and many scientists may come to join Horton in thinking it practically advisable. If one needs to put it this way, the independence of science has got cash value.

Finally, the obverse of scientists living down to expectations that they will do whatever they can get away with is the possibility that they will live up to a renewed presumption that they are honest, disinterested, and incorruptible. Accordingly, it would be good for scientists themselves to express greater outrage when commerce corrodes disinterestedness, to accept whatever shrinkage in their resources might come from the limitation of compromising commercial ties, and to speak more openly, and less embarrassedly, in front of their colleagues and students about science as a calling. I'd be happy to trust such scientists to use their expertise disinterestedly, since their moral authority would be everything that is possible for late modern technical experts.

Endnotes

[1] Steven Shapin, *A Social History of Truth: Civility and Science in Seventeenth-Century England,* Chicago: University of Chicago Press, 1994, ch. 1; see also idem, 'Trust, Honesty, and the Authority of Science', in *Society's Choices: Social and Ethical Decision Making in Biomedicine,* Ruth Ellen Bulger, Elizabeth Meyer Bobby, & Harvey V. Fineberg (eds), for Committee on the Social and Ethical Impacts of Developments in Biomedicine, Institute of Medicine, National Academy of Sciences, Washington, DC: National Academy Press, 1995, pp. 388–408.

[2] See Charles R. Thorpe, 'Disciplining Experts: Scientific Authority and Liberal Democracy in the Oppenheimer Case', *Social Studies of Science* 32, 2002, pp. 525–562.

[3] See, for example, Ruth Shalit, 'When We Were Philosopher Kings: The Rise of the Medical Ethicist', *The New Republic* 216, no. 17, 28 April 1997, pp. 24–28; Carl Elliott, 'Diary', *London Review of Books* 24, no. 23, 28 November 2002: 'Bioethics rests on a thin layer of public trust that can easily be shattered. Full-disclosure policies may help that process along. Once bioethics becomes publicly identified as a tool for industry, its practitioners may face a choice between going back to their old jobs in the philosophy department or signing up for new corporate positions as risk managers and compliance officers.'

[4] See the views of two of the 20th century's most articulate research managers, Ken Mees and John Leermakers of Eastman Kodak, e.g. C. E. Kenneth Mees and John A. Leermakers, *The Organization of Industrial Scientific Research,* 2nd ed., New York: McGraw-Hill, 1950, p. 14; John A. Leermakers, 'Basic Research in Industry', *Industrial Laboratories* 2, no. 3, March 1951, pp. 2–3: 'It is in the universities that true intellectual freedom, so essential to the development of the scientific attitude, is found.' I recall similar opinions about academic research independence expressed during the Thatcher years by Sir John Harvey-Jones of ICI.

Contributors

Pervez Hoodbhoy is Professor of Physics at Quaid-e-Azam University, Islamabad where he has taught for over 30 years. He holds a PhD in nuclear physics from the Massachusetts Institute of Technology and is the recipient of several awards including the Abdus Salam Prize for Mathematics, the Baker Award for Electronics, and the UNESCO Kalinga Prize for the popularisation of science. He is Visiting Professor at MIT, Carnegie Mellon University, the University of Maryland and often lectures at US and European universities and research laboratories. Dr Hoodbhoy is involved in social issues as well, such as women's rights, environment, education, and nuclear disarmament. He is author of *Islam and Science: Religious Orthodoxy and the Battle for Rationality*, now in five languages, and has made video documentaries on the India–Pakistan nuclear issue as well on the Kashmir conflict. He is frequently invited to comment on South Asian politics in Pakistani and international media.

Daniel Glaser is an imaging neuroscientist and Senior Research Fellow at the Institute of Cognitive Neuroscience, University College London. He uses fMRI (functional magnetic resonance imaging) to examine human brain function and how experience, prejudice and expectation alter the way we see the world. He comes from an unusual academic background: he studied mathematics and English literature at Cambridge, achieved a Master's in cognitive science at the University of Sussex, and followed this with graduate work in neurobiology. In 2002 he was appointed first 'Scientist in Residence' at the Institute of Contemporary Arts (ICA) in London, where he collaborated with the ICA curators to put on talks, hold panel discussions, and conduct psychological experiments. He has made numerous radio appearances, featured in newspaper and net articles, and chairs the ICA's Café Scientifique. Daniel is interested in finding novel ways for scientists to collaborate with arts practitioners and engage with the public.

Steven Shapin is Professor of the History of Science, joining Harvard in 2004 after previous appointments as Professor of Sociology at the University of California, San Diego, and at the Science Studies Unit, Edinburgh University. His books include *Leviathan and the Air-Pump: Hobbes, Boyle, and the Experimental Life* (Princeton University Press, 1985; with Simon Schaffer), *A Social History of Truth: Civility and Science in Seventeenth-Century England* (University of Chicago Press, 1994), and *The Scientific Revolution* (University of Chicago Press, 1996; now translated into 14 languages). He has published widely in the historical sociology of scientific knowledge, and his current research interests include historical and contemporary studies of dietetics, the nature of entrepreneurial science, and modern relations between academia and industry. He is working on a book about scientific expertise and personal virtue in late modern America, and has received several awards including the J. D. Bernal Prize for career contributions to the field.

Lloyd Anderson is the British Council's Director of Science, Engineering and Environment, based in Manchester, UK. He holds a first degree in Botany from Imperial College London, a PhD in Plant Physiology from Lancaster University and has published over 60 scientific papers and articles. In his current job, he is responsible for setting corporate policy in science, engineering and environment in close consultation with major UK stakeholders and partners; helping to translate that global policy into strategies at the regional and local level. With science network representatives in 60 countries, he ensures that British Council teams overseas promote British science innovatively and effectively. He works at senior level within the UK science community and Whitehall to build understanding and support for the British Council's science work, and is a member of the British Association for the Advancement of Science, British Ecological Society, the Institute of Biology, and an Associate of the Royal College of Science.